Cause and Effect,

the Political Redemption

Mohammed Abdullah

PAGE PUBLISHING, INC.
New York, NY

First originally published by Page Publishing, Inc. 2018

ISBN 978-1-64214-367-6 (Paperback)
ISBN 978-1-64214-369-0 (Hardcover)
ISBN 978-1-64214-368-3 (Digital)

Printed in the United States of America

CONTENTS

CHAPTER 1

Reasoning and Procedure of Law

One fundamental principal of law is that law is inerrant. When societies begin to accept error enforcement, social order becomes void, as well does all things pertaining to law, such as justice, morality, sanity, righteousness, and purpose of human existence!

A government is not a person or a building or an assembly of military equipment. A government is an ideology which people govern themselves accordingly.

Jurisprudence can only be justified when the punishment is equal to the crime, and the benefit of the doubt is sanctioned by compensation or restitution! The act of impartiality and objectiveness when exercising law and judgment is a characteristic of high achievement! Ignorance, arrogance, and egoism are methods used by human beings to portray themselves as adversaries to law! The idea of a person having enmity toward another person or a people having enmity toward another people is a mental illusion!

Our actions determine whether we are enemies to wickedness, corruption, evil, wrongfulness, stupidity, and anarchy or whether we are enemies to law! It is the epitome of arrogance for man to conceive the notion that he is a maker of law! The essence of law is defined as divine intervention or divine law or cause and effect.

Man is not the inventor of cause and effect; man is a product of cause and effect!

Agreements and ordinances between humans that are not based on divine law result themselves to vanity! To debate facts pertaining to law, by questioning the validity of the term, is the same as questioning all the things that define law, such as reality and existence, right and wrong, good and bad, order and chaos, morality and immorality, ethics and perversion, etc.

The act of declaring uncertainty when referring to law is not a venue to legitimize skepticism. Law is not subjected to the approval or disapproval of man! Law is an entity of absoluteness and cannot be controlled by man. Neither can law be made subordinate to the likes and dislikes of human beings! Law is a mechanism of activity that has been established far beyond man's proximity as well as the cosmos and the nebula! To insinuate that law is questionable or obscure or outdated, does delete one iota of sovereignty ordained unto it by the Creator of it. Intelligence or knowledge is not to be taken for granted, and proof can only be concluded by application or testing! All human beings are obligated to test information for the sake of integrity. So for those who are interested in seeking knowledge pertaining to law and the information pertaining to it are afforded an unlimited amount of starting places to begin testing, such as the laws of gravity, the laws of aging, the laws of birth and death, and the multiple laws of nature, etc.

Instead of exhibiting enmity when addressing issues attributed to law, it is more practical to say, "I have tested such and such attributes to law, and found it to be true or false!" Then after all human efforts are applied and exhausted, all honor and glory are due to the majesty and lord and creator of law, and we are to be forever grateful for being given life and the privilege of living according to law. To *vote* in favor of a political party or a policy or mandate that promotes injustice is a *vote* for social injustice, self-degradation, and mental dereliction!

CHAPTER 2

Capitalism vs. the Proclaimed Laws of God

Capitalism, an ideology of government that is contemporarily based on private business, which controls the manufacturing and production and the distribution of goods. It is a bureaucracy that has existed for thousands of years and has continued to evolve despite the rise and fall of the civilizations that have used it as their form of government. Also capitalism has been used as a target for antics and criticisms for thousands of years, by adversaries ranging from philosophers to professors to religious groups from all denominations!

Capitalism has been deemed the covert motivation behind imperialism and oppression, terrorism and slavery, chaos and famine, treachery and social manipulation, and political decadence. Capitalism has been diagnosed as one of the leading causes of mass psychological mental disorders and suicide.

Capitalism has been classified as the provocateur of the increased crime rate within the society and the exploitation immoral behavior.

These are analyses that resonate from within the social litigants chronological evidence. Nevertheless, just as capitalism is no stranger to longevity, neither is it an irony that capitalism is no stranger to negative language. It would be an aberration to think that idealisms that withstand the test of time are without substance. The thing that gives epoxy to an ideology is not aspirations alone. It is the practicalities of the idea that makes it whole! Capitalism does not define itself as the moral majority; neither do the constituents of capitalism hesitate to admit that the system is not perfect! Capitalism is business oriented. It is an ideology whose principal concepts are based on pragmatism! It is an act of vanity to hold the ideology of capitalism responsible for the failures of the world! It is just as much a vanity to give benediction to capitalism for all the good things of the world. Capitalism has been for thousands of years a subject of antagonism and propagation. For many years among many civilizations, capitalism also has been promoted as the symbol of power and prosperity! Capitalism has been attributed as the cause for producing one of the most powerful militaries in the world! Capitalism has been revered as the cause for the manufacturing of unprecedented amounts of materials and goods. Capitalism has been held as the bright light shining the path to which the pursuit of happiness became visible! Despite the controversy pertaining to capitalism, it remains an institution of influence and dominance. Then there's the issue of specifics like crime and punishment and the question of its logic and feasibility from a business perspective. Is it feasible to have a penal system that is financially non-self-sufficient? Is it feasible to postpone a trial because of a lack of evidence? Is it ethical from a judicial perspective for a judge presiding over a hearing to grant a continuance on behalf of insufficient evidence? Is it in the name of logic that a judge should participate in a plea bargaining or is it an indication that the integrity of the judicial process is on sale? Should equity be the norm when enforcing justice, or is it ambiguous to define crime and punishment as unequal? Is it ethical to invent a law and exact punishment to those who break the law, then abolish the law and offer no reimbursement to those who were punished in vain? Is there such a thing as a judicial process that is so profuse in wit that it can afford negligence and ill-afford account ability? Is it a sacrilege to make a declaration of allegiance to a written constitution that promotes genocide? Or should the defiance of treachery be considered an act of treason or is it a breach of sanity to claim that no one can be sure about the subject of right and wrong? Or is it feasible to institutionalize guilt by employing mercenaries to enforce obscurity? Are we as human beings obligated to affirm within ourselves the absoluteness of law? Should we as human beings negate our responsibility of knowing law in order to justify cowardice, vain conformity, and persecution? True affirmation of knowledge is to act according to it; which oftentimes gives incentive to socially discard laws such as eye for an eye, tooth for a tooth, murder for murder, wound for wound, limb for limb, etc.! These are laws written also by the hands of men, just as the laws pertaining to capitalism were written by men! The difference between these writings is that one has been proclaimed by men as divine scripture and the others have not. The belief of these proclamations are discretionary matters! The essence of law is its practicalities and its moral effectiveness! The differences of opinions regarding authenticity of words are a forfeiture of the true purpose or literature! It is not the source of literature that constitutes the validity of its contents, be they true or false! It is the contents of literature and the meaning of its composition that validates the authenticity and verification of origin! The truth is self-evident and is the conveyor of its own origin and its own certification and its own authenticity and its own proof! Falsehood is by definition an illusion and is therefore without origin or existence!

Therefore, when questions arise as to whether a script is divine or whether it is from God or man, it is in reality, not an issue of origin but an issue relating to mental capacities and comprehension skills or the laws pertaining to rape and the castration of the rapist and whether this is a law given to man from God or an idea invented by man! Consider the law pertaining to capital punishment! It is the avoidance of divine purpose that breeds insane behavior among human beings and the psychic denial of divine consequence! Is it an issue of confusion or controversy among human beings as to what is right and what is wrong? Or is it a constant excuse for the human being to give reason to satisfy his relentless ego? Morality is not a fantasy or a myth that can be altered or modified in order to comply with social preference or moral subordination! Or is it armed robbery and the amputation of the hand that was used by the robber to commit the crime? Or is it the notion of claiming belief in God and the proclaimed doctrines of God but declare opposition to capital punishment! It is the avoidance of divine purpose that breeds insane behavior among human beings and the psychic denial of divine consequence!

CHAPTER 3

Violence, War, and Terrorism

War and terrorism are activities that are never found one without the other. War is often described as deadly, violent, bloody, vicious, petrifying, horrifying, and terrible! Despite mass killings and atrocities of great proportion, man has of yet been unable to eliminate war, but has ironically increased his war capacity to mega, astronomical proportions! Throughout the history of mankind, war, violence, and terrorism have often been used as a means of settling disputes and resolving problems. Due to man's massive participation in war and due to man's feverish development of weaponry and equipment to make war clearly demonstrates man's ability to employ his lesser skills to resolve problems than his greater skills to resolve them, such as preventing war by employing the application of intelligence! When the means to eliminate war is by the escalation of war, then the end will not justify the means. As long as violence and terrorism are used as primary resources to resolve problems, war will forever remain! War, violence, and terrorism cannot be eliminated by only the use of tangible artifice. It is because war, violence, and terrorism are manifestations of those which are intangible, which is human ideologies!

The lack of knowledge and ignorance are the origins of human conflict and human error. War is a temporary approach to resolve human conflict, but it is far from being a remedy! And how should we define terrorism? Is it just a method used in war, or is it a behavior by definition? Such as when a child disrespects its parent, that's terrorism! When a parent abuses his or her child, that's terrorism! Armed robbery is terrorism! Rape is terrorism! Racial profiling is terrorism! Spousal abuse is terrorism! Carjacking is terrorism! Intimidation is terrorism! Degradation is terrorism! Slavery is terrorism! Oppression is terrorism! Violence, war, and terrorism are not confined to land boundaries, ethnical backgrounds, or political agendas. War, violence, and terrorism are home-based within the human brain and submerges when the circumstance provides the opportunity. All of the physical manifestations of war are evident proofs of man's ability to use his God-given willpower to bring war, violence, and terrorism into existence! Therefore, if man has the ability to create war, violence, and terrorism, then surely man has the ability to withdraw them from existence!

It is an insult to human intelligence to declare that utopia does not exist. When a child shows honor and respect to his or her parent, that's utopia! When a parent fulfills his or her parental duties unto his or her child, that's utopia! When a human being treat's another human being with respect, that's utopia! Any act of goodness and sanity is a manifestation of utopia! And it is we humans who ought to be ashamed of ourselves if it were not utopia on Earth. And if it were not any evidence of utopia, there would be no human existence on Earth because we will self-destruct!

How difficult is it to shift blame or to compromise validity in exchange for a lifetime of living in denial? Who are *they*, that portray themselves as authority but refuse to rid themselves of social corrosion? Plea bargaining within the judicial system and so-called law enforcement are terrorism! Entrapment within so-called law enforcement is terrorism! Bail-bonding within the so-called justice department and law enforcement is extortion, obstruction of justice, and social-political terrorism! For example, it is appalling for a judge who is to preside over a hearing to ask the person accused of a crime to plead guilty to a lesser crime in exchange for a lesser sentence without having a fair trial, which as a result pollutes the judicial process and demotes the judge's credibility due to the abandonment of impartiality! It is an injustice to charge an innocent person a fine or a fee in terms of a bond in defense of their innocence! It is an injustice to allow a guilty person to go free on bond before retribution or restitution, regardless of their guiltiness after the fact! It is a travesty of justice to state in a court of law that the amount of the bond is according to the severity of the charge. Meanwhile the plight of the victim and the judicial process are polarized! Unlawful acts and immoral behavior are the ingredients that make the recipe of war, violence, and terrorism!

CHAPTER 4

Love, Marriage, and the Science of Family

Love, marriage, and the family are the rainbow of human existence and social aggrandizement! Love is a term within the English language that describes human emotion, passion, and feelings of heartfelt desire. Love has often been the primary motivation of man in life. Love has often been the inspiration for high achievement's and accomplishments of greatness and sacrifice! Despite all the goodness that has also been attributed to love, it has also been a thing often attributed to man's demise due to man's tendency to love things without regard to reason or outcome! The end results prove that love is an emotion that's most beneficial when it is governed by reasoning, objectiveness, and a criteria that's based on moral judgment. Love is an emotion of complexities that multiply when human beings come together in marital or spousal relationships! Love is a major factor in the participation of human relations! Love has also been used as a basis in which men and women have built their relationships on, and again the end results prove that love is not enough to fortify or found a relationship! Marital and spousal relationships that are founded on principles are enhanced and energized by the combination of both love and principle! Marital and spousal relationships that are without principles leave room for corrosion within the moral fiber of society. Relationships not based on principles open a way for divorce, disease, prostitution, fornication, adultery, homicide, illegitimate childbirth, and a decadent, exploitative breakdown of the family unit within society! The ideal concept of marriage is that it is for the purpose of human reproduction and the continuance of human existence!

Marriage is not limited to the joining together of a man and a woman. Marriage is also the joining together of families as well as nations! Neither is marriage limited to human relationships of love and companionship. It is also applied in various realms of life, such as business and principalities and law. When a business or a corporation merges with another business or corporation, it is a marriage. When a person makes a vow to devote his or herself to a criteria of law, it is a marriage, and it is due the same amount of effort and devotion! The concept of family is not just an accumulation of trends that acknowledges ties of blood and kinship and love within the family. It is the responsibility of all humans to develop their morally refined people-skills into a science!

Another concept of marriage and family is polygamy. Polygamy is a marriage of one man and multiple woman. It is a method; that the criteria is also governed by the fundamental principles of morality! Evidence proves that societies that have a low-percentage rate in crimes such as murder, rape, sodomy, prostitution, abortion, child abandonment, fornication, adultery, robbery, child abuse, vandalism, and war often rank high in the percentage rate of marriage. Societies that have low-percentage rates in marriage rank high in disease, divorce, suicide, and mental disorders! Marriage is a social and moral obligation. The science of family is a social and moral obligation, and love is a gift from God!

CHAPTER 5

The Putridity of Self-Righteousness in So-Called Religion

The putridness of self-righteousness in so-called religion is a demonstration of overt sacrilege of divine instructions and a desecration of common sense! Self-righteousness among human beings in the name of religion is an exercise of irrelevance in human behavior! It is the paramount of insignificance and an audacity of vanity and self-glorification, that a human being should declare as self-righteousness. Is it not an insult to intelligence that the proclamation of self-piety supersedes merit? The use of words and titles do not constitute the validity of merits. The actions and deeds of human beings speak for itself and are self-evident with or without the support in verbatim! Personal adjuration by religious denominations does not guarantee righteousness! All human beings are subjected to divine law regardless of claims of piety. Righteousness when displayed in a form of human behavior is based on good deeds and is subject to change according to changes within the person or group of people.

For example, in the Arabic language, there is a pronoun derived from the verb and root word *aslama*, which means submission. The word Muslim is a noun, which is the name of a person, place, or thing that is in submission. When the term Muslim is used in reference to divine instructions, the meaning is that which is in submission to God or the Creator! By definition of the term, everyone and everything in the heavens or the universe is a Muslim, regardless of molecular structure. The term Muslim does not constitute merit; neither is the term Muslim confined to ethnic background, symbolic rituals, or verbal oaths! There is no such thing as a non-Muslim! There is no such thing as taking an oath to become a Muslim! Everyone and everything is a Muslim by reason of existence. Therefore, when people use the term Muslim out of context by saying, "I'm this kind of Muslim or that kind of Muslim," it is unnecessary and is a statement without merit! For example, the word Christian is a pronoun that is derived from the adjective and root word Christo from the Greek language, which means *nobility* or the Anointed. In the modern-day English language, it is defined as Christ-like. When the term Christian is used out of context by saying, "I'm this kind of Christian or that kind of Christian," it is an unnecessary statement and does not constitute merit! Or is it noble to use words and titles to distinguish one's self in the eyes of people at the expense of divine instructions? Or is it an act of virtue to declare an oath of allegiance to a particular sect or denomination? If so, then why do all religious sects and denominations make this claim? Has the priority of humans in reference to divine instructions become a congregation of fraternities and sororities, engaging in spiritual competition?

Despite all of the claims of self righteousness, to claim to be a certain kind of Christian is unnecessary and does not constitute merit. Despite all of the claims of self-righteousness from so-called religious denominations, hatred, bitterness, bloodshed, antagonism, and war result from the proliferation of religious competition. Religion is often defined as a way of life, culture, or system of belief. The term religion is usually associated with worship, God, and spirituality. It is not God who is to blame; neither is the instructions of God to blame; human beings are to blame because of the putrid inventions of false deities, false religions, false cultural concepts, false saints, false prophets, false doctrines, and false reasons for participation! To obey God does not require an oath of allegiance to a human being, a group of beings, a particular sect or denomination, and not even a particular school of thought! Also there is no such thing as converting from one religion to another. The conversion from one religious denomination to another does not have any bearing on the divine law; neither does divine law convert to accommodate the uncertainties of man! Likewise, the term unity or social harmony in reference to divine law does not limit its criteria to symbolic forms of unity! The term unity is an ideology in which it functions accordingly! Is it not possible to have people gathered in a group, but they are against each other? The essence of unity is best exemplified by having people that are far from each other in geographical distance, language, and culture but function according to the same ideology!

Or the example of two separate building contractors that are given identical blueprints of a structure, both builders follow the same instructions and the unity is demonstrated by their results, being that the structures they have built are identical at the completion of them! The worst among all putridity of self-righteousness in religion is paganism, idolatry—the worship of idols, and the attribution of false things to God!

CHAPTER 6

Social Bias

Social bias, an issue far from the magnitude of major, has without cease been orchestrated and promoted by mentalities within society as if it's an issue of such proportion that resolve cannot be attained! Never in the history of man has a problem in its beginning stage started large! All problems begin small and develop in size by human apparatus. A key element within all human societies that cannot afford distortion is diplomacy, which is the science of communication, reasoning, and comprehension—to be adroit when it comes to language and behavior!

For example, an estimation to one man can be a calculation to the next man. Is it biased or a freedom of choice? All decisions are according to objectiveness. It is a habit among human beings to tend to love a thing that could be bad and hate a thing that could be good! Favoritism is a human right that must be respected as long as it is not used to violate the rights of others. If the terms, bias, prejudice, favoritism, etc., are used to violate the rights of others, then the terms and their definitions will change and become immoral! Social bias when demonstrated in forms of abuse takes root within the consciousness of the human being!

Social bias in the form of abuse has the ability to transform itself in all realms of society and has the ability to disguise itself in many forms, such as nationalism, patriotism, gender, genealogy, economics, academics, ethnicity, religion, and political, industrial, judicial, and ghetto biases!

Another example, nationalistic bias is when a nation of people deem themselves as superior to existing nations outside of their geographical boundaries! Patriotic bias is when a person is willing to kill or die on behalf of their country regardless of moral justification. Gender bias is when a male or a female person violate and abuse the rights of the other because they are of the opposite sex.

Genealogical bias is when a person or a people deem themselves superior to others because of their birthright, bloodline, or ancestry. Economic bias is when the distribution of wealth is altered to benefit or deprive a person or a people despite moral justification. Academic bias is when the educational institutions alter teachings or hinder access to a particular knowledge in order to serve an immoral agenda. Ethnic bias is when a person or a people violate the rights of another person or people because of differences in culture, language, social background, or physical appearance! Religious bias is when a religious doctrine, person, or people transgress the laws of Divinity and abuse the rights of others because of differences in religious practice. Political bias is when a person or people violate the rights of another person or people because of a difference in political agenda or political point of view.

Industrial bias is when an industry abuses the rights of others and the natural environment and produce or hinder production of goods in order to benefit or deprive, without moral justification.

Judicial bias is when a judicial process abuses authority and violates the rights of others by transgressing the boundaries of law. Ghetto bias is when a person or a group of people violate the rights of another person or a people because one lives or resides in different sides of town.

There are two kinds of victims, innocent victims and volunteer victims. Most people are volunteer victims. Those who violate the rights of others using biased methods will become a victim of their own premeditation!

CHAPTER 7

A Tribute to Cosmopolitan

It is a term defined as having the ability to relate to all parts of the world, having the world as one's country, free from national prejudice. This writing is to pay tribute to all who know and understand the profoundness of this term and who live within the essence of its meaning and those who dare not live by any other social status!

It is articulated by a world-renowned musician, "Until that day, the dream of lasting peace world citizenship and the rule of international morality will remain but a fleeting illusion to be pursued, but never attained now everywhere is war—war."

It means that the day will come when all people are respected, not viewed as foreigners or aliens. The day will come when all citizens of the world will live according to the basic, fundamental principles of morality, when all the stereotypical ideologies pertaining to nationalism and eth-nic identity is removed from the focus point within the social consciousness!

The cosmopolitan is one who does not limit himself or herself to local affairs; neither is the cosmopolitan hin-dered by diversity of environment, language, or culture.

International citizenship is the apex of civilization! It is formidable that a person's character is his or her identification as opposed to a landmass or a dialect. Within the subconscious of the human is a need for confirmation of self, and it is only them who have attained this confirmation of self have the ability to embody the mentality of the cosmopolitan! Those who are void of self-affirmation are unable to orbit this realm of intelligence! Those who lack self-affirmation tend to identify themselves by what is called relatedness. Relatedness in reference to identity is the act of a person identifying themselves by comparison and association to things other than themselves. Also the lack of self-affirmation extends to subjected peer pressure, social manipulation, and group conformity; the reason being the need of acceptance, a sense of belonging, and the approval of others to measure their own self-worth!

Also, those who lack self-affirmation, tend to employ the method of deindividualization whenever appropriate, in order to invent justification for a wrongdoing unto another person. The act of deindividualization is when a perpetrator, within his or her own mind, removes the identity of its victim by viewing its victim as nobody, worthless, not sacred, and insignificant! Those reasons mentioned are proofs why the mental concept of cosmopolitan is a necessity! We are obligated as one humanity to employ the mental concept of cosmopolitan, and it is our responsibility as human beings to pay tribute and respect to all those who are vanguards and implementers of the mental intellect defined as cosmopolitans!

EIGHT SPEECHES TO THE WISE

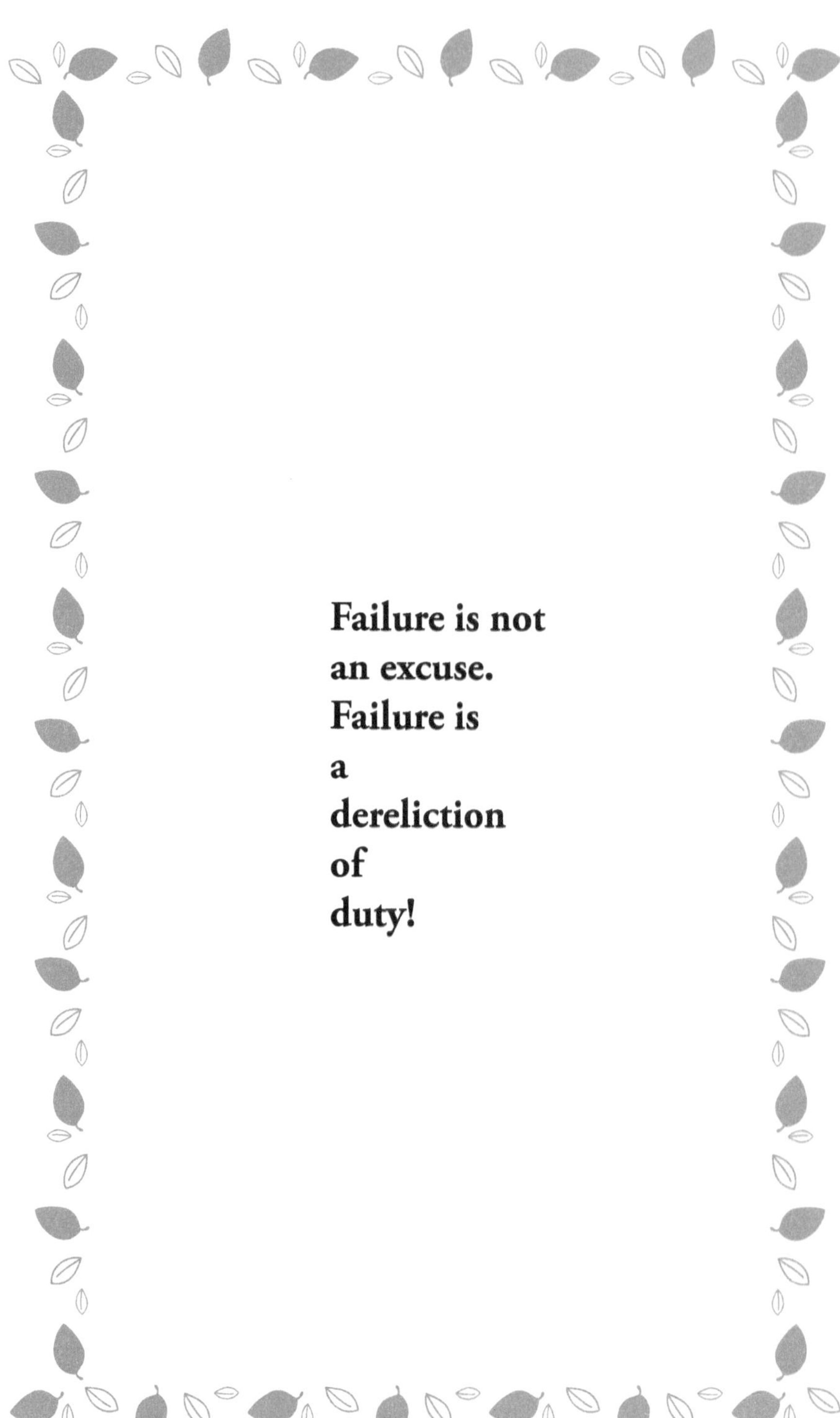

Failure is not
an excuse.
Failure is
a
dereliction
of
duty!

**No
job or job title
can give prestige to a man.
A man must bring
prestige
to the job!**

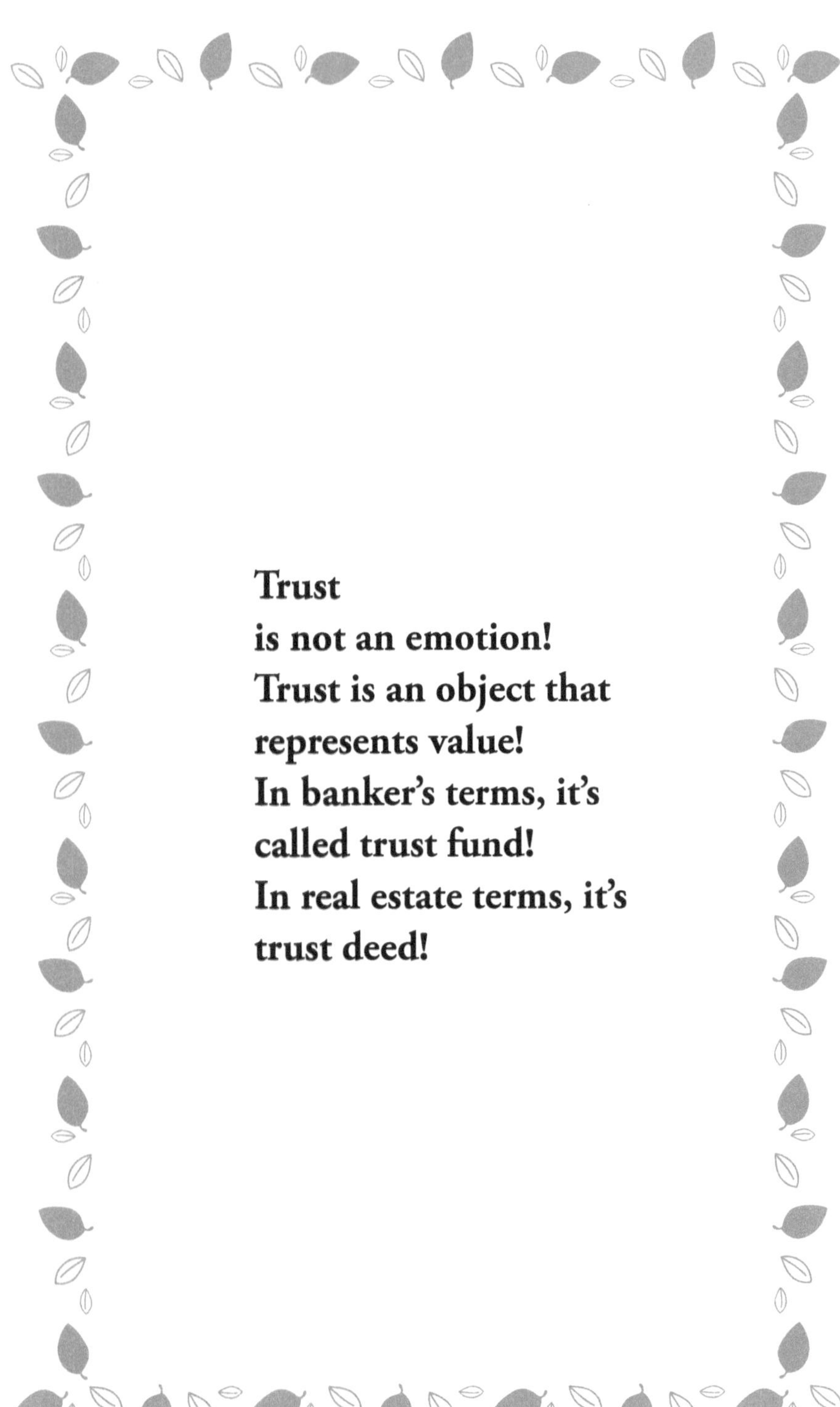

Trust
is not an emotion!
Trust is an object that
represents value!
In banker's terms, it's
called trust fund!
In real estate terms, it's
trust deed!

Respect
comes before
love!
Respect is a given!
Disrespect
is
earned!

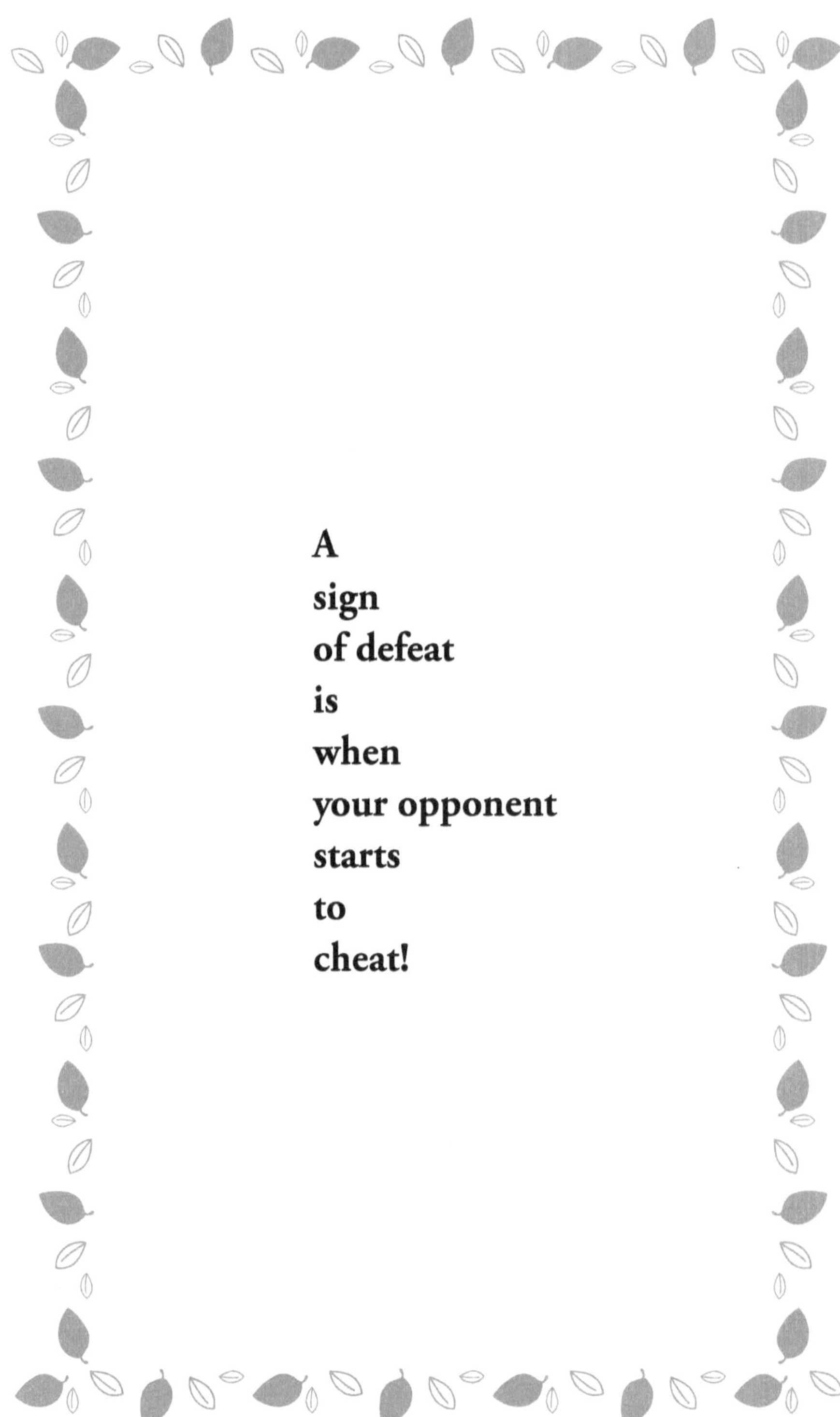

A
sign
of defeat
is
when
your opponent
starts
to
cheat!

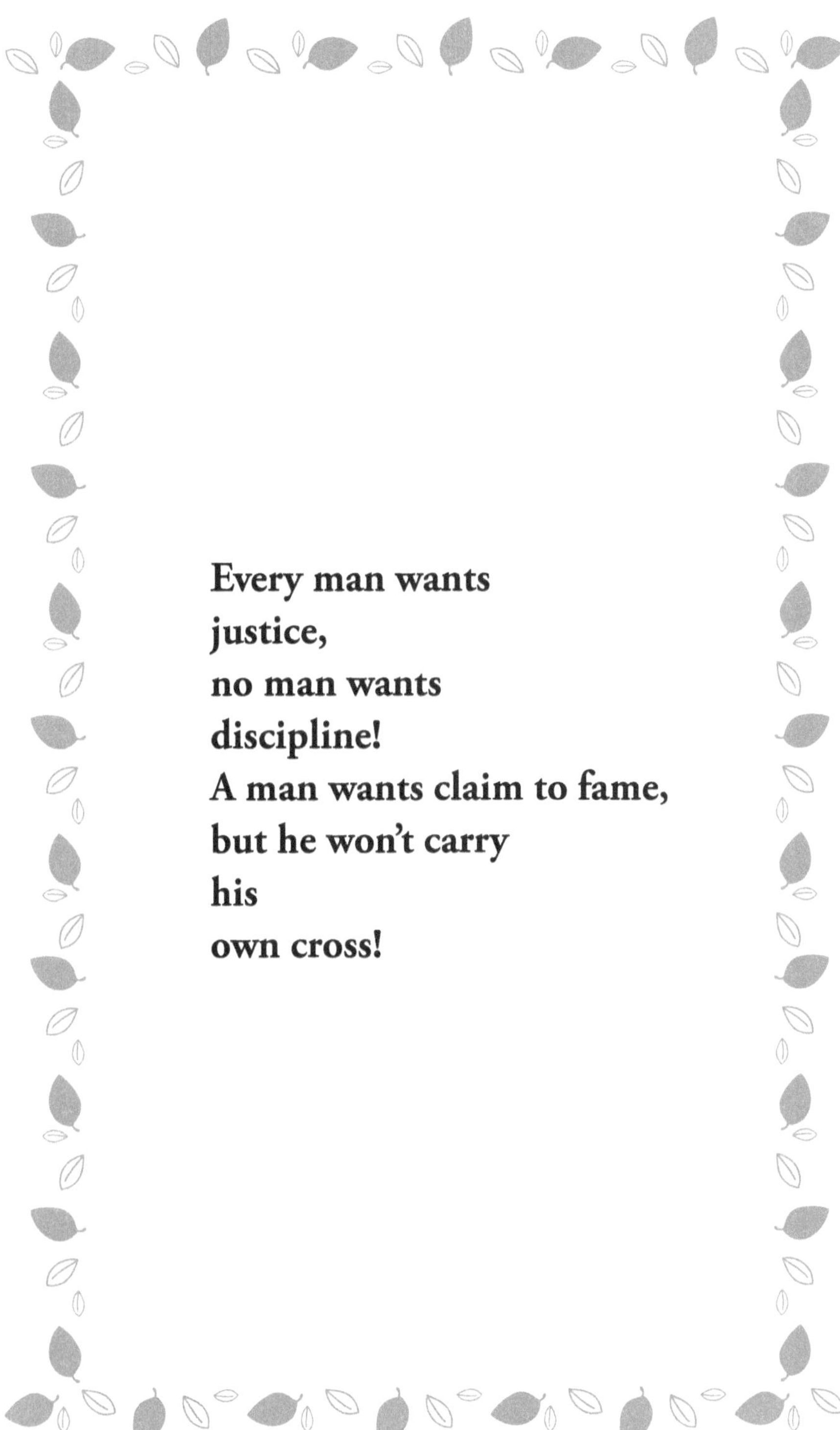

Every man wants
justice,
no man wants
discipline!
A man wants claim to fame,
but he won't carry
his
own cross!

the Lesser
the expectations,
the
smaller
the disappointment!

The
reward
for
conformity
is
the approval
of
others!

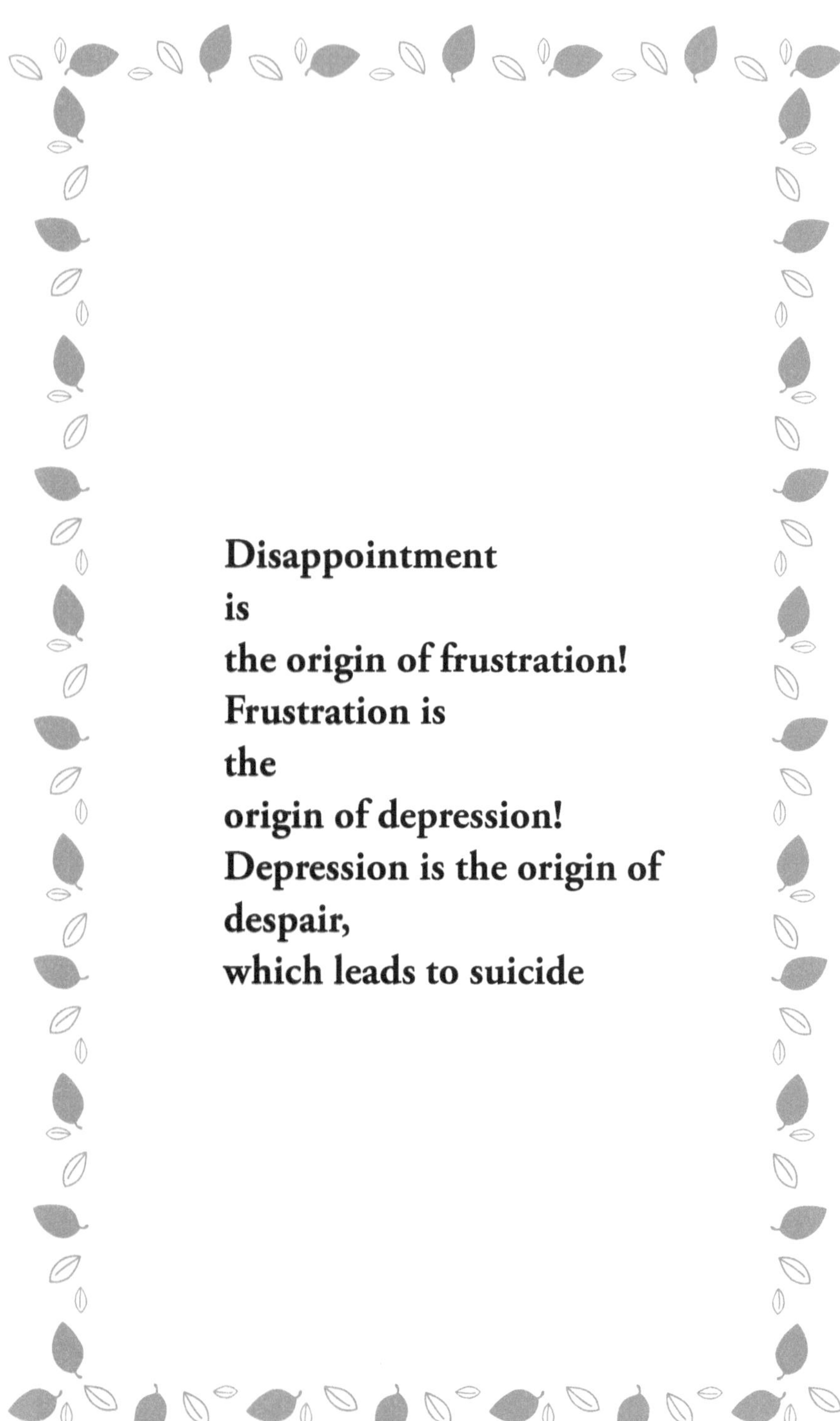

Disappointment
is
the origin of frustration!
Frustration is
the
origin of depression!
Depression is the origin of
despair,
which leads to suicide

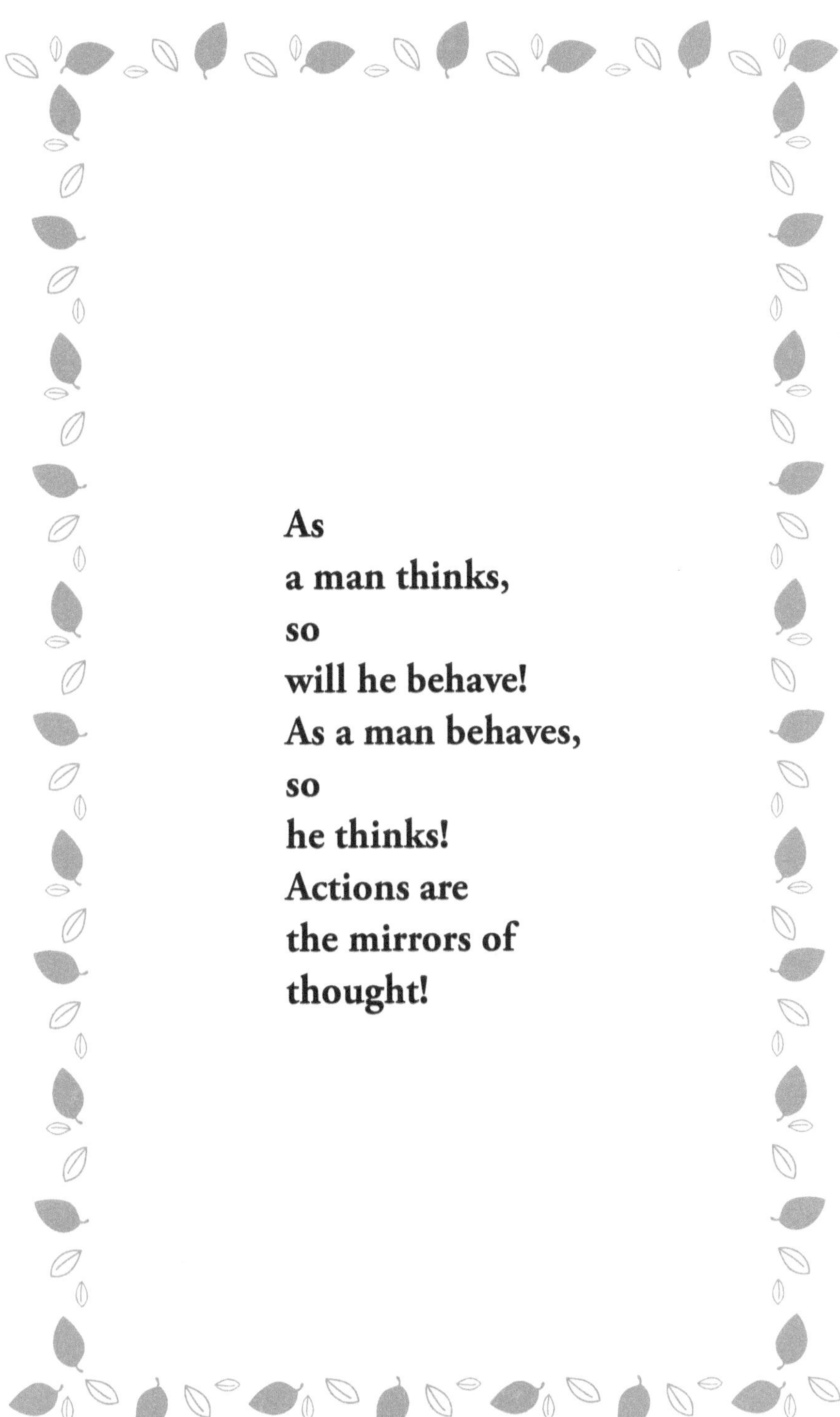

As
a man thinks,
so
will he behave!
As a man behaves,
so
he thinks!
Actions are
the mirrors of
thought!

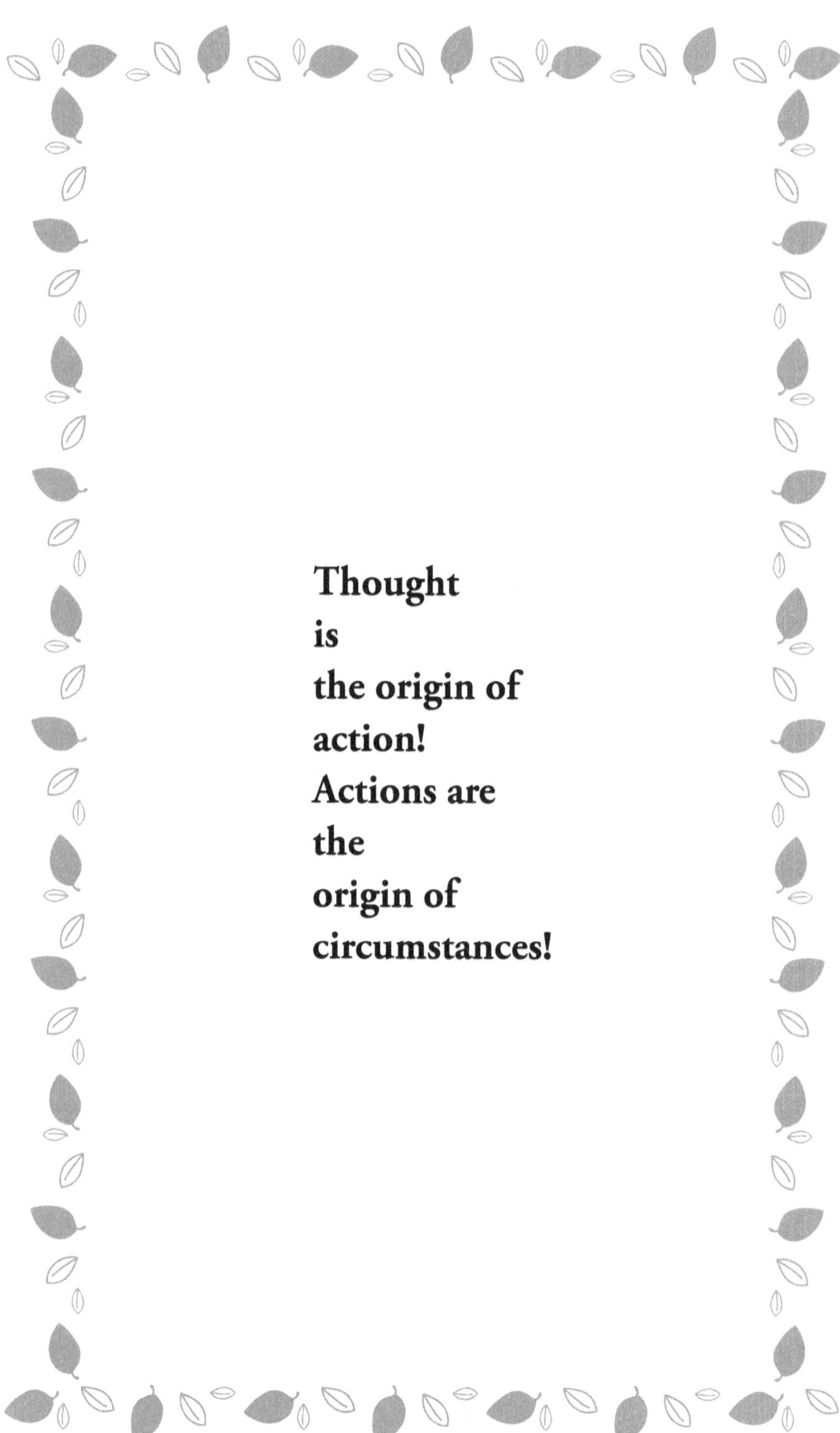

**Thought
is
the origin of
action!
Actions are
the
origin of
circumstances!**

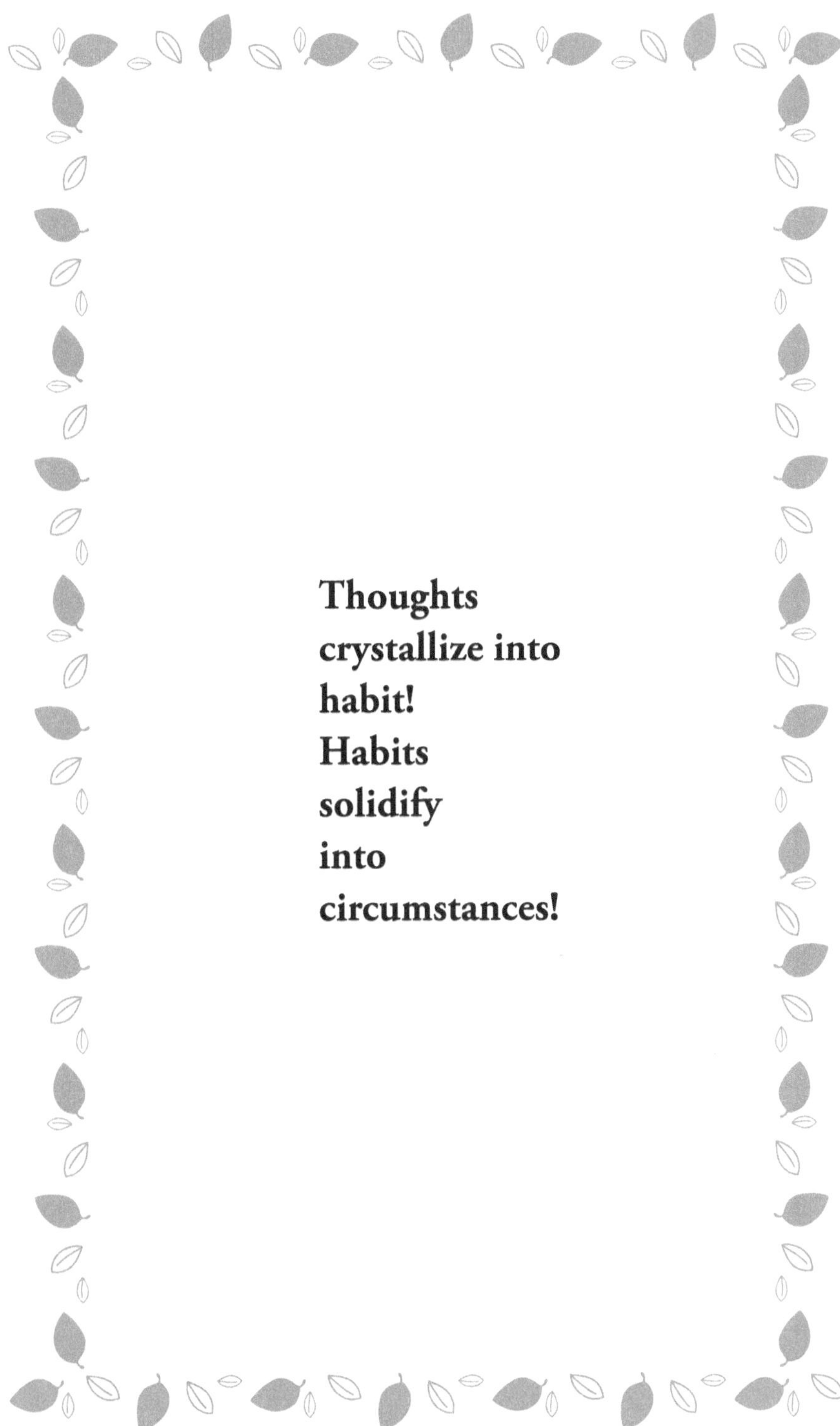

**Thoughts
crystallize into
habit!
Habits
solidify
into
circumstances!**

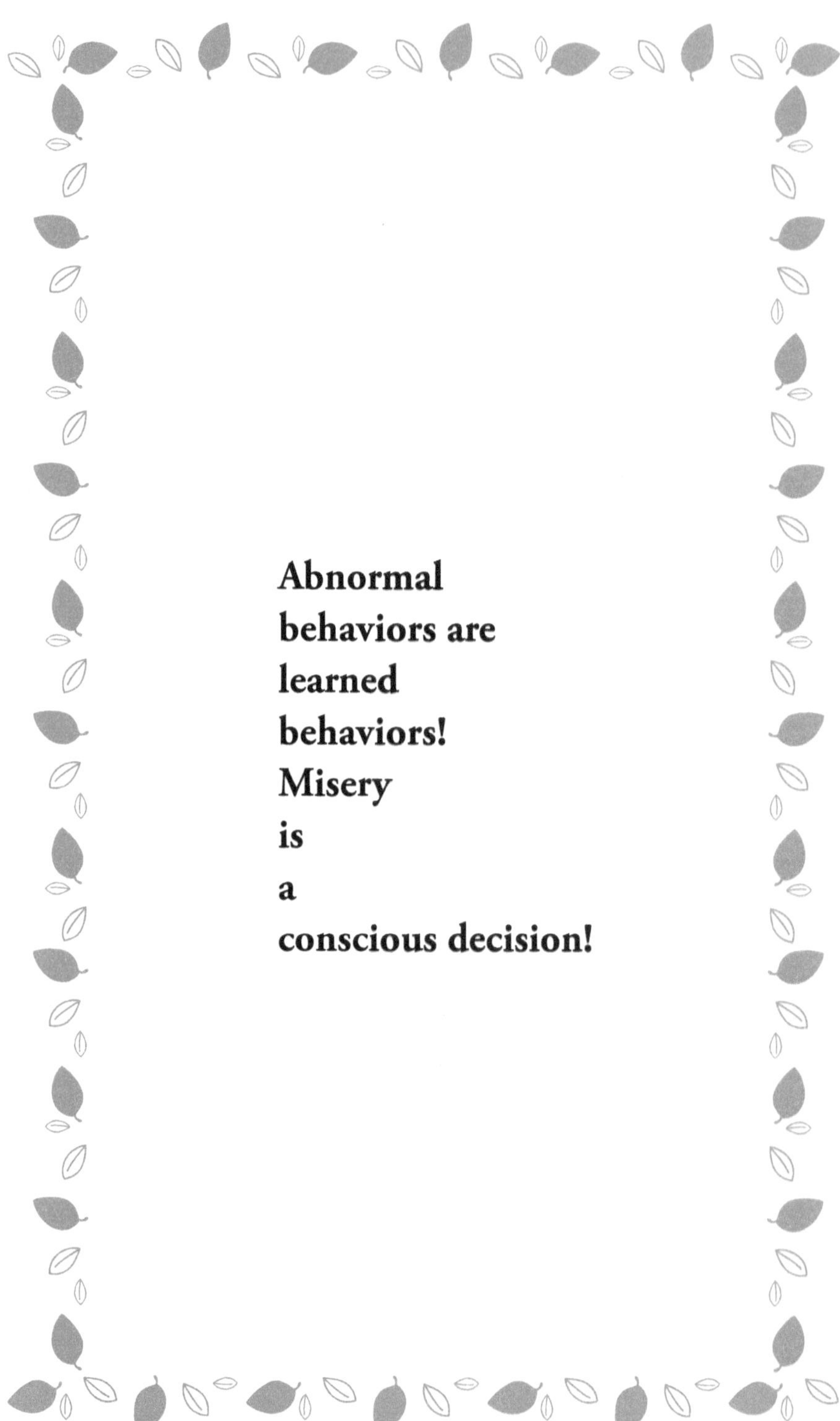

**Abnormal
behaviors are
learned
behaviors!
Misery
is
a
conscious decision!**

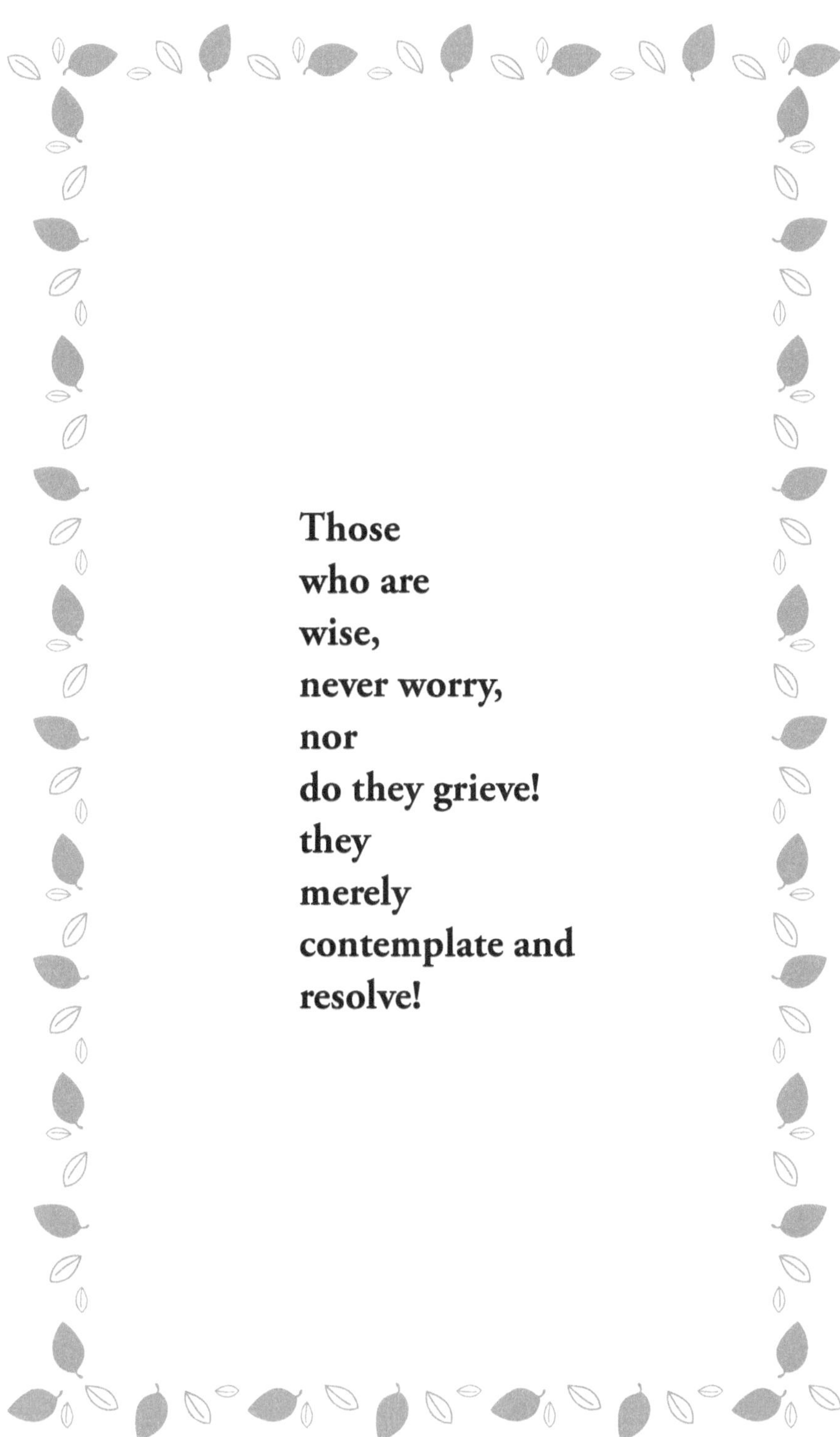

Those
who are
wise,
never worry,
nor
do they grieve!
they
merely
contemplate and
resolve!

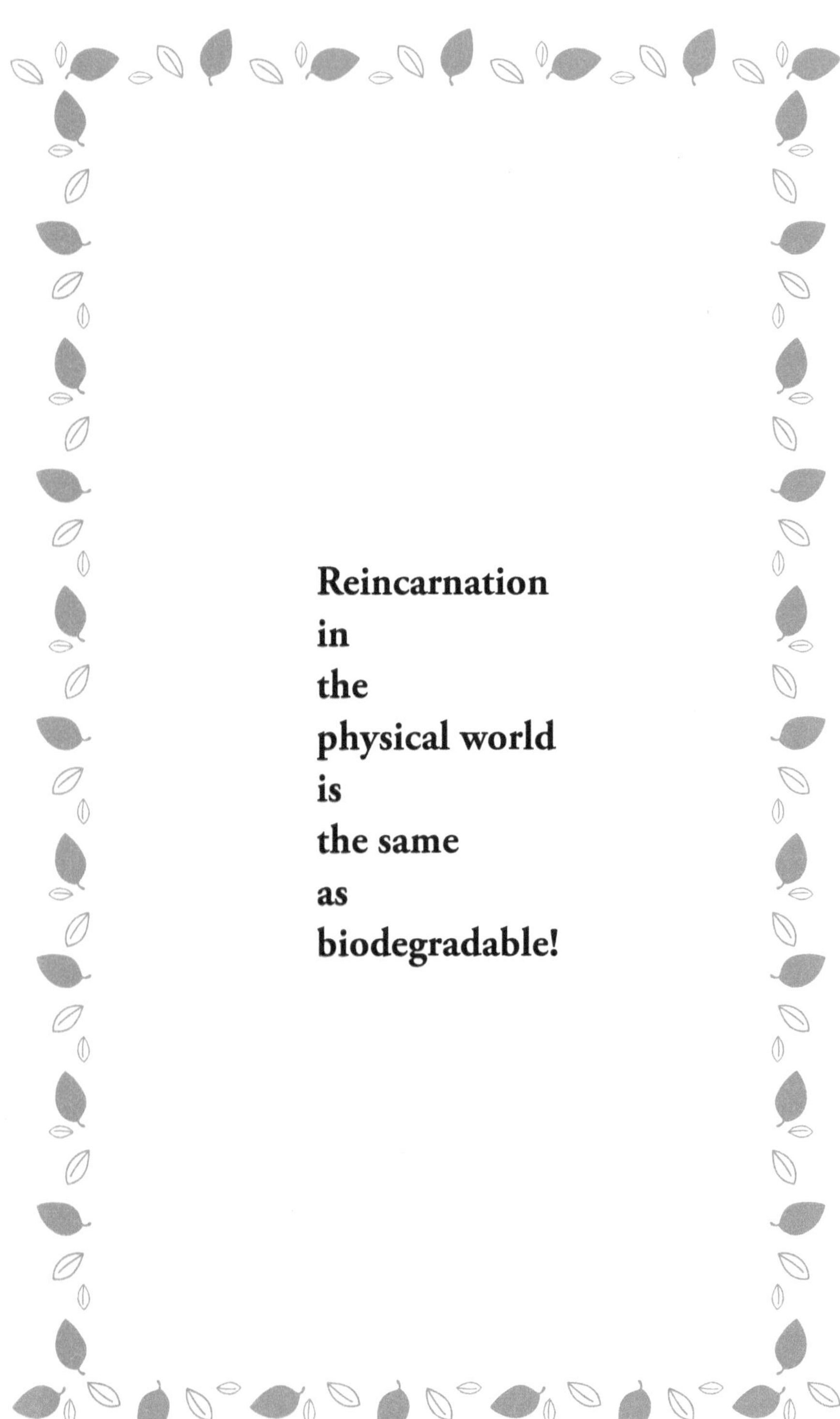

**Reincarnation
in
the
physical world
is
the same
as
biodegradable!**

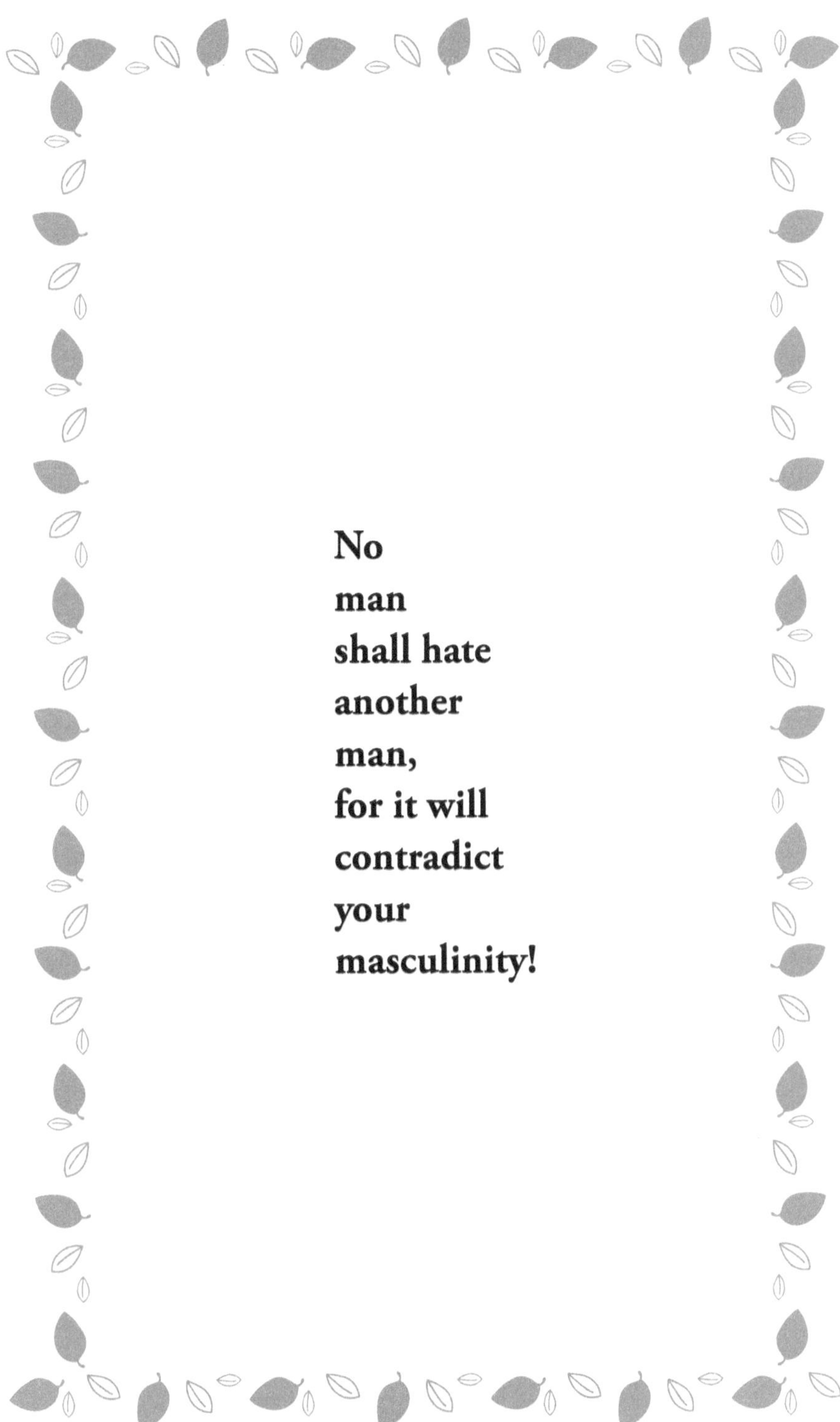

No
man
shall hate
another
man,
for it will
contradict
your
masculinity!

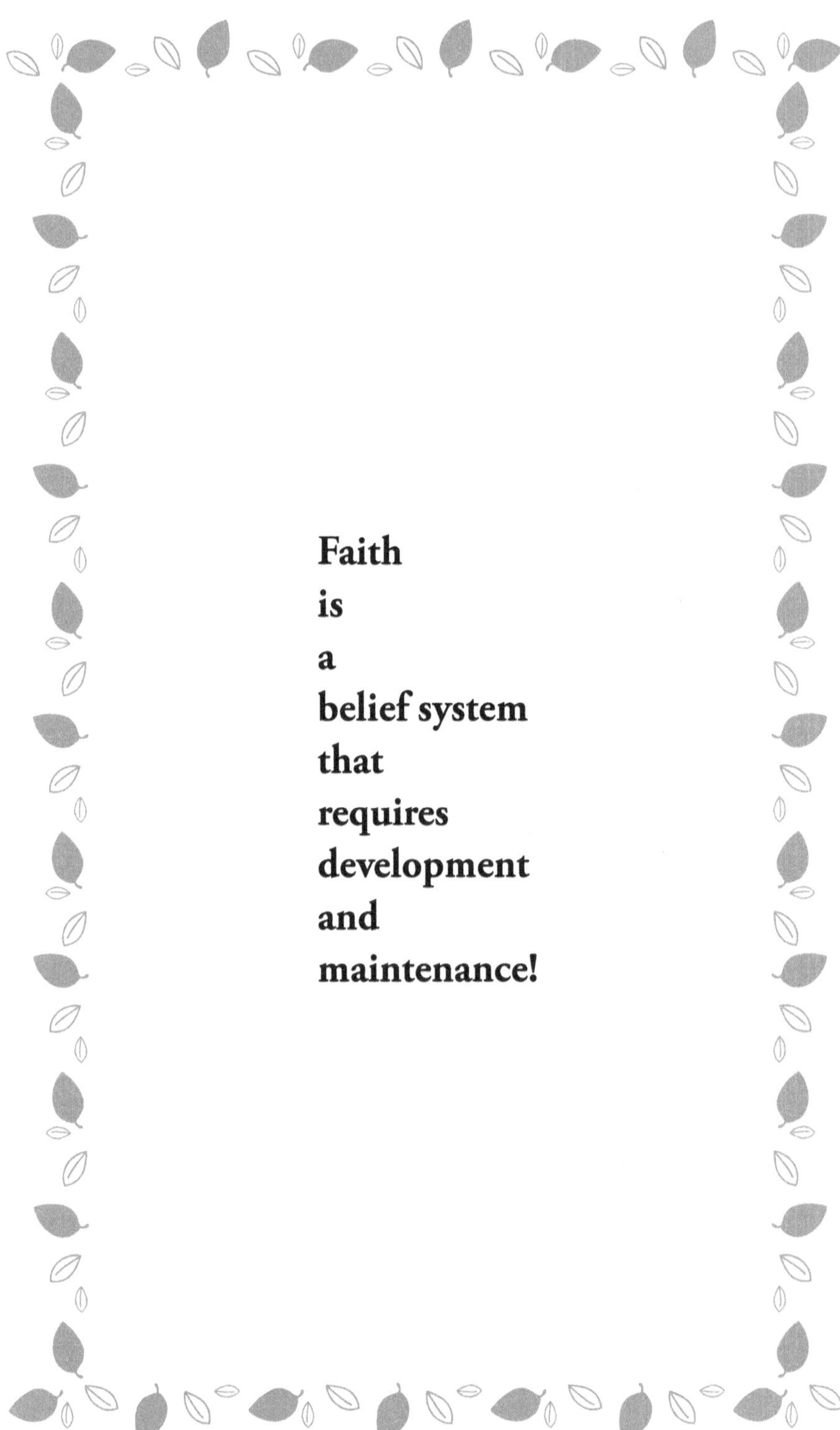

Faith
is
a
belief system
that
requires
development
and
maintenance!

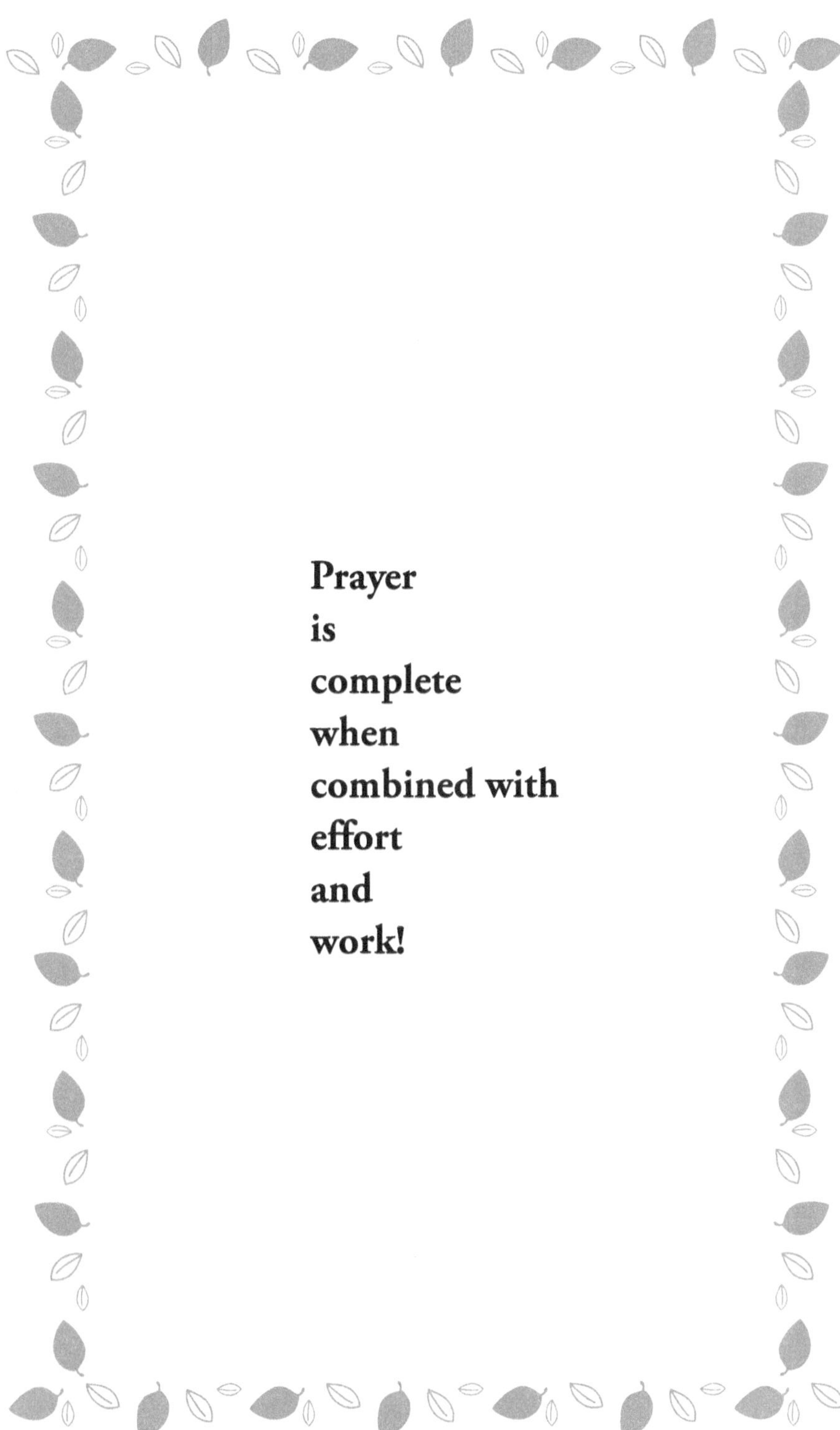

Prayer
is
complete
when
combined with
effort
and
work!

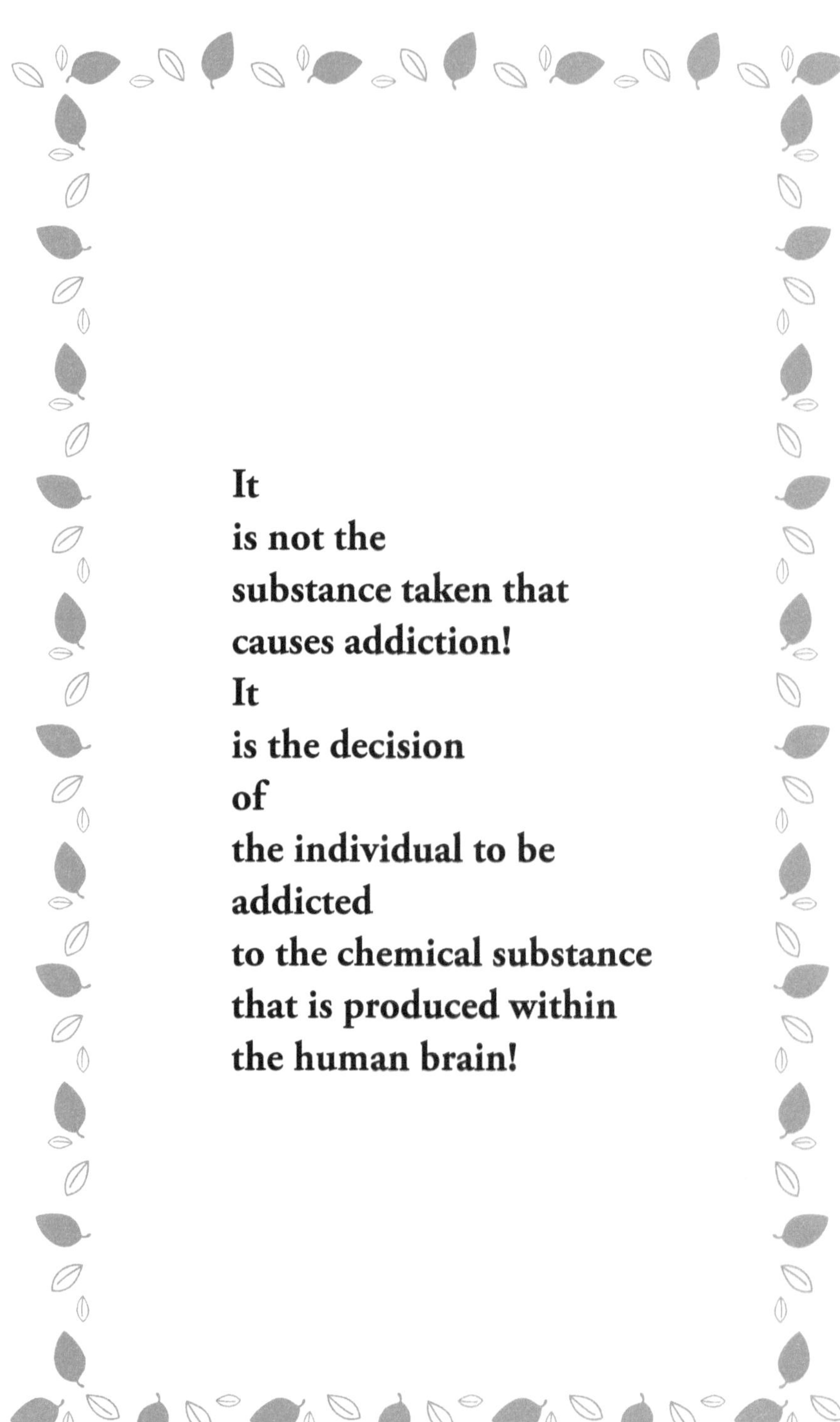

It
is not the
substance taken that
causes addiction!
It
is the decision
of
the individual to be
addicted
to the chemical substance
that is produced within
the human brain!

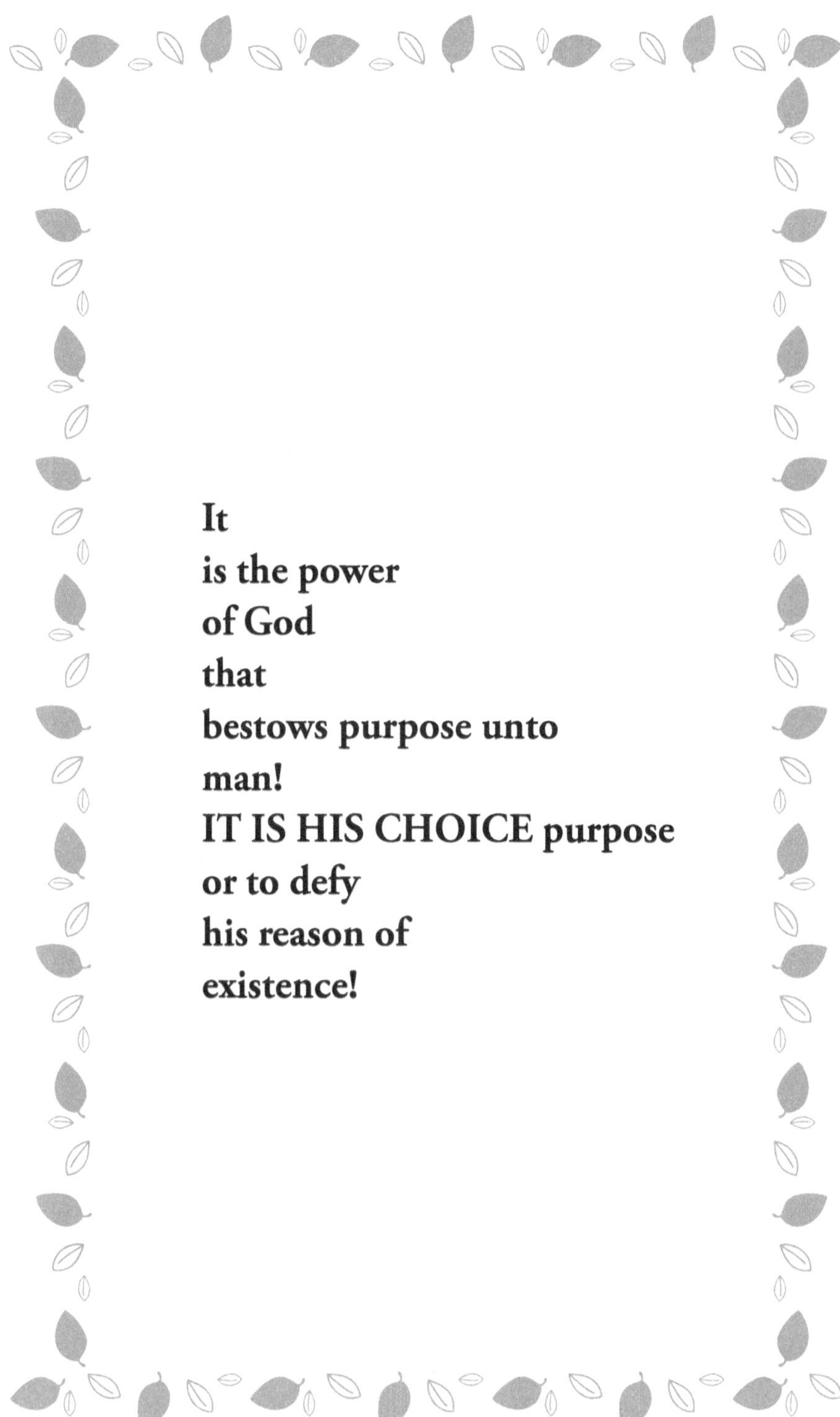

It
is the power
of God
that
bestows purpose unto
man!
IT IS HIS CHOICE purpose
or to defy
his reason of
existence!

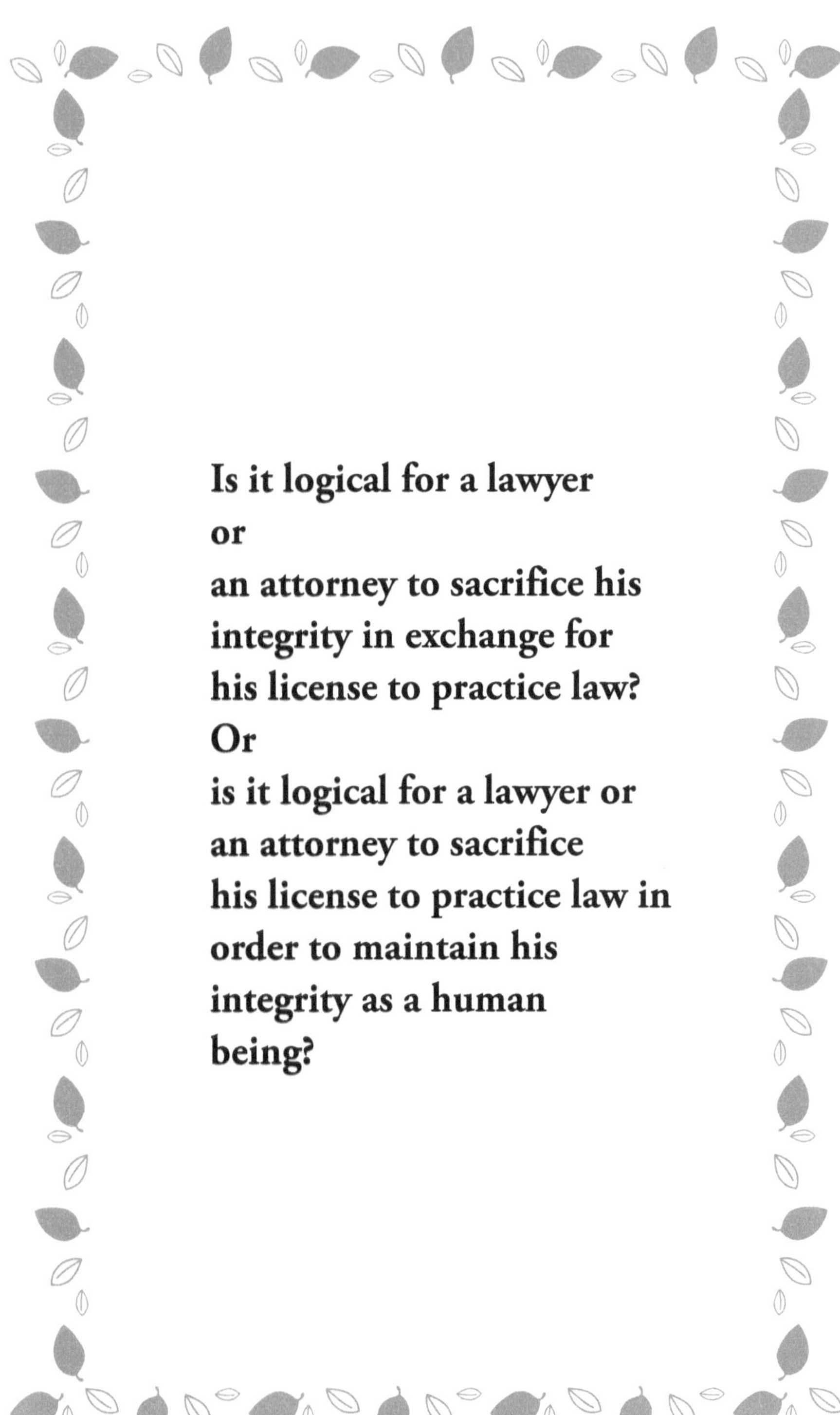

Is it logical for a lawyer
or
an attorney to sacrifice his
integrity in exchange for
his license to practice law?
Or
is it logical for a lawyer or
an attorney to sacrifice
his license to practice law in
order to maintain his
integrity as a human
being?

ABOUT THE AUTHOR

Mohammed Abdullah is self-employed. He sells incense and oils, and music is his passion. He is grateful to Page Publishing for providing the opportunity to authors like himself and others.